see and say

guarda e parla
regarde et parle
mira y habla

a picture book in four languages

guarda e parla   mira y habla

see and say

regarde et parle

woodcuts by

antonio frasconi

a voyager book

harcourt brace jovanovich, inc., new york

para pablo

*Uno solo es lo que ves
aunque te parezcan mas que tres.*

Since I was brought up in a home where more than one language was spoken, I was given at an early age the knowledge that there is more than one nation and one way of speaking in our world. The idea that there are many nationalities speaking many languages is to me one of the most important for a child to understand.

See and Say has grown from this belief and from my experience and personal need in living with and teaching my son Pablo.

Beside each object pictured in this book you will find the word for it in English, Italian, French, and Spanish, together with a guide to the pronunciation. The following color key has been used throughout: ● Black for English words; ● Blue for Italian words; ● Red for French words; ● Green for Spanish words. There is also a page of everyday expressions all children use.

A.F.

ISBN 0-15-680350-X

sun

sun

sole

soh-láy

soleil

soh-láy-ee

sol

sohl

chicken   **pollo**

chik-n   poh-loh

poulet   **pollo**

poo-lay   poy-oh

tree   **albero**   **arbre**   **arbol**

tree   áhl-bay-roh   ahr-br   áhr-bohl

houses
how-zes

case
kah-zay

maisons
may-zong

casas
kah-sas

egg
eg

uovo
oo-óh-voh

oeuf
uf

huevo
wáy-voh

bridge
bri-j

ponte
póhn-tay

pont
pohng

puente
pwen-tay

rose
ro-z

rosa
róh-sah

rose
ro-z

rosa
róh-sah

grasshopper
grás-hop-ur

cavalletta
kah-vahl-lét-tah

sauterelle
soh-te-rél

saltamontes
sal-tah-móhn-tays

suitcase
sóot-kayss

valigia
vah-lée-jah

valise
vah-leess

valija
vah-lée-hah

snail
snayl

lumaca
loo-máh-kah

escargot
es-kar-goh

caracol
kara-kól

bus
bus

autobus
ah'oo-toh-boos

omnibus
ohm-nee-beus

autobus
ah'oo-toh-boos

ants
ants

formiche
for-mée-kay

fourmis
foor-mee

hormigas
or-mée'-gahs

sheep　　**pecora**　　**mouton**　　**oveja**
sheep　　páy-koh-rah　　moo-tóhng　　oh-váy-hah

chair
chair

sedia
sáy-de'ah

chaise
shez

silla
séel-yah

elephant
éle-funt

elefante
ay-lay-fáhn-tay

éléphant
ay-lay-fahng

elefante
ay-lay-fáhn-tay

night
nyt

notte
nóht-tay

nuit
nwee

noche
nóh-chay

book
book

libro
lée-broh

livre
lee-vr

libro
lée-broh

corn
kohrn

grano
gráhn-oh

maïs
mah-ées

maiz
mah-éeth

girl
gurl

ragazza
rah-gáht-sah

fille
fee-ee

muchacha
moo-cháh-chah

cow
kow

vacca
vah-kah

vache
vah-sh

vaca
vah-kah

hand   *máhn-oh*   *ma-'ng*   *máhn-oh*

hand   mano   **main**   mano

barn   granaio   **grange**   granero

bahrn   *grah-náh-e'oh*   *grahnj*   *grah-náir-oh*

grapes
gráy-pss

uva
óo-vah

raisins
ray-zang

uvas
óoh-vahs

cat
kat

gatto
gah-toh

chat
sha

gato
gah-toh

automobile
áw-toh-moh-beel

automobile
ah'oo-toh-móh-bee-lay

automobile
oh-toh-moh-béel

automóvil
ah'oo-toh-móh-veel

wheel   ruota   roue   rueda

hweel   *roo-óh-tah*   *rooh*   *rwáy-dah*

lion   leone   lion   león

ly-on   *lay-óh-nay*   *lee-ohng*   *lay-óhn*

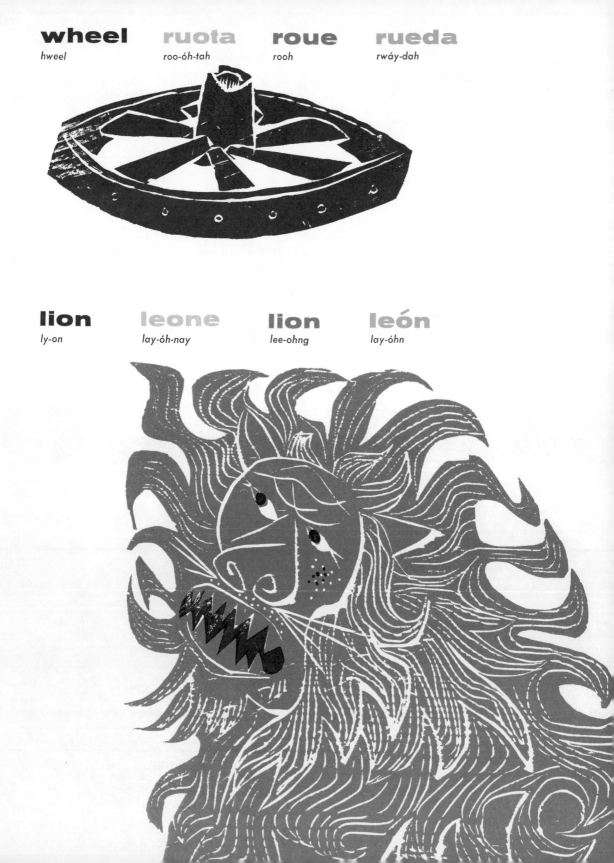

wind
wind

vento
ven-toh

vent
vahng

viento
vee-én-toh

whale
hwayl

balena
bah-láy-nah

baleine
bah-len

ballena
bal-yáy-nah

fishermen

fish-ur-men

pescatori

pess-kah-tóhr-ee

pêcheurs

peh-sheur

pescadores

pess-kah-dór-es

sea

see

mare

máh-ray

mer

mair

mar

mahr

anchor

ánk-or

ancora

ahn-kóh-rah

ancre

ahng-kr

ancla

áhn-klah

Christmas tree
Kris-mus tree

albero di Natale
áhl-bay-roh dee Nah-táh-lay

arbre de Noël
ahr-br duh Noh-el

árbol de Navidad
áhr-bohl day nah-vee-dáhd

tomato **pomodoro**
to-máh-toh *poh-moh-doh-roh*

tomate **tomate**
toh-máht *toh-máh-tay*

cake **torta**
kayk *tohr-tah*

gâteau **torta**
ga-toh *tohr-tah*

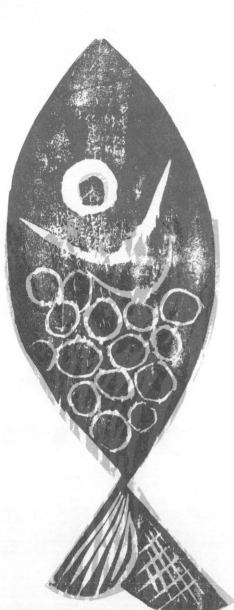

boat
boht

barca
bár-kah

bateau
bah-toh

barco
bar-koh

fish
fish

pesce
pé-shay

poisson
pwa-sohng

pescado
pes-káh-doh

hat
hat

cappello
kah-pél-loh

chapeau
sha-póh

sombrero
som-bráir-oh

school
skoohl

scuola
skoo-óh-lah

école
ay-kul

escuela
es-ku-áy-lah

airplane

áir-playn

aeroplano

ah-ay-roh-pláh-noh

aéroplane

air-oh-plan

aeroplano

ah-ay-roh-pláh-noh

horse

hors

cavallo

kah-váhl-loh

cheval

shu-val

caballo

kah-bál-yoh

fly
fly

mosca
mos-kah

mouche
moo-sh

mosca
mos-kah

peas
peez

piselli
pee-zél-lee

pois
pwah

guisantes
ghee-sán-tays

dog
dawg

cane
káh-nay

chien
sh'eyng

perro
pér-roh

shoes
shooz

scarpe
skár-pay

souliers
sool-yea

zapatos
thah-páh-tos

bed
bed

letto
lét-toh

lit
lee

cama
káh-mah

goat
goh-t

capra
kah-prah

chèvre
she-vr

cabra
kah-brah

train
trayn

treno
tráy-noh

train
treyng

tren
trayn

bird
burd

uccello
oo-chéll-oh

oiseau
wah-zóh

pájaro
páh-ha-roh

cup   **tasse**   **taza**
kup   táht-tsah   tass   tah-thah

rain
rayn

pioggia
pee-óh-ja

pluie
plwee

lluvia
lyoó-vee-ah

umbrella
um-brél-ah

ombrello
om-brél-oh

parapluie
pah-rah-plwee

paraguas
pah-ráh-gwas

light
lyt

luce
loo-chay

lumière
leum-yair

luz
looth

butterfly
bút-ur-fly

farfalla
far-fáhl-lah

papillon
pah-pee-yong

mariposa
ma-ree-póh-sah

table
táy-bl

tavola
táh-voh-lah

table
tah-bl

mesa
máy-sah

pig **porco** **cochon** **cerdo**
pig *por-koh* *koh-shóng* *ther-doh*

grass **erba** **herbe** **hierba**
gras *air-bah* *air'b* *yair-bah*

farmer
fár-mur

fattore
fah-tóh-ray

fermier
fair-mee-ay

labrador
lah-brah-dór

turkey
túr-kee

tacchino
tahk-kée-noh

dindon
dehng-dohng

pavo
páhv-oh

world
wuhrld

mondo
món-doh

monde
mohn-d

mundo
mun-doh

clouds
klowd-z

nubi
noo-bee

nuages
neu-ahj

nubes
noo-bes

numbers
núm-burz

numeri
nóo-may-ree

nombres
nohng-br

números
nóo-may-ros

ladder
lad-ur

scala
skáh-lah

échelle
ay-shel

escalera
es-kah-láir-ah

See and Say
see and say

Happy birthday!
hap-pee burth-day

I love you!
i luv yoo

Merry Christmas!
máir-ee kris-mus

My name is_____.
my naym iz

What a beautiful day!
hwat ay byoo-te-ful day

How are you?
how ahr yoo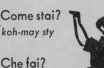

What are you doing?
hwat ahr yoo doo-ing

Let's have lunch.
lets hav lunch

What time is it?
hwat tym iz it

Good morning!
good móhr-ning

Good night!
good nyt

Good-bye!
good-by

Let's go!
lets goh

Happy New Year!
hap-pee nyoo yeer

That's all.
thats awl

Guarda e Parla
gwar-dah ay par-lah

Buon compleanno!
bwohn kom-play-áh-noh

Ti voglio bene!
tee vohl-yoh bay-nay

Buon Natale!
bwohn nah-táh-lay

Mi chiamo_____.
mee kee-áh-moh

Che bella giornata!
kay bél-ah jur-náh-tah

Come stai?
koh-may sty

Che fai?
kay fy

Facciamo colazione.
fatch-ee-áh-moh
koh-láh-zee-óh-nay

Che ora è?
kay óh-rah ay

Buon giorno!
bwohn jor-noh

Buona notte!
bwohn-ah noh-tay

Arrivederci!
ah-rée-veh-der-chee

Andiamo!
ahn-dee-ah-moh

Buon Anno!
bwohn ah-noh

E questo é tutto.
ay kwes-toh ay too-toh

Regarde et Parle
re-gard ay parl

Joyeux Anniversaire!
jwa-euze ah-nee-vair-sair

Je t'aime!
szhuh tem

Joyeux Noël!
jwa-uh noh-él

Je m'appelle_____.
szhuh mah-pel

Quelle belle journée!
kel bel szhur-nay

Comment vas-tu?
koh-mahng vah-too

Que fais-tu?
kuh feh-too

Allons déjeuner.
a-lohng day-shzeu-nay

Quelle heure est-il?
kel eur et-teel

Bon jour!
bohng szhuhr

Bonne nuit!
bun nwee

Au revoir!
oh rev-wahr

Allons!
a-lohng

Bonne Année!
bun ahn-nay

C'est tout.
say too

Mira y Habla
mee-rah ee ah-blah

¡Feliz cumpleaños!
fay-léeth koom-play-
áh-nyos

¡Te amo!
tay áh-moh

¡Felices Navidades!
fay-lée-seth
nah-vee-dáh-dez

Me llamo_____.
may lyáh-moh

¡Qué hermoso día!
kay air-móh-soh dée-ah

¿Cómo estás?
koh-moh ess-táhs

¿Qué haces?
kay áh-sess

Vamos almorzar.
vah-moh, ah al-mor-zar

¿Qué hora es?
kay óh-rah ess

¡Buenos días!
bway-nohs dée-ass

¡Buenas noches!
bway-nahs nóh-chess

¡Hasta la vista!
ah-stah lah vee-stah

¡Vámonos!
váh-moh-nohs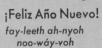

¡Feliz Año Nuevo!
fay-leeth ah-nyoh
noo-wáy-voh

Esto es todo.
ess-toh ess toh-doh

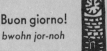
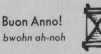